# The **Hudson** River

by Ian Wood

**Gareth Stevens Publishing**
A WORLD ALMANAC EDUCATION GROUP COMPANY

**Please visit our web site at: www.garethstevens.com**
**For a free color catalog describing Gareth Stevens Publishing's list of high-quality books and multimedia programs, call 1-800-542-2595 (USA) or 1-800-387-3178 (Canada). Gareth Stevens Publishing's fax: (414) 332-3567.**

Library of Congress Cataloging-in-Publication Data

Wood, Ian.
 The Hudson River / by Ian Wood.
  p. cm. — (Rivers of North America)
 Includes bibliographical references and index.
 Contents: Gateway to the northeast—From source to mouth—The life of the river—River of many nations—From freight to fun—Places to visit—How rivers form.
 ISBN 0-8368-3755-X (lib. bdg.)
 1. Hudson River (N.Y. and N.J.)—Juvenile literature. [1. Hudson River (N.Y. and N.J.)]
I. Title. II. Series.
F127.H8 W95 2003
974.7'3—dc21            2003042742

This North American edition first published in 2004 by
**Gareth Stevens Publishing**
A World Almanac Education Group Company
330 West Olive Street, Suite 100
Milwaukee, Wisconsin 53212 USA

Original copyright © 2004 The Brown Reference Group plc. This U.S. edition copyright © 2004 by Gareth Stevens, Inc.

Author: Ian Wood
Editor: Tom Jackson
Consultant: Judy Wheatley Maben, Education Director, Water Education Foundation
Designer: Steve Wilson
Cartographer: Mark Walker
Picture Researcher: Clare Newman
Indexer: Kay Ollerenshaw
Managing Editor: Bridget Giles
Art Director: Dave Goodman

Gareth Stevens Editor: Betsy Rasmussen
Gareth Stevens Designer: Melissa Valuch

Picture Credits: Cover: Verrazano Narrows Bridge. (Skyscan: Jim Wark)
Contents: Leisure boat on the Hudson River in Westchester County, New York.

Key: l–left, r–right, t–top, b–bottom.
Ardea: P Morris 12; Corbis: 17, 18, 28; Bettmann 5t, 15, 19, 29b; Dean Conger 22; Lowell Georgia 10; E. O. Hoppé 21; James Marshall 5b; Joe McDonald 11; Gail Mooney 29t; David Muench 6; Richard T. Nowitz 20; Joseph Sohm; ChromoSohm Inc. 8/9; David H. Wells 26/27; Dutchess County Tourism: 13t, 23; Getty Images: Peter Gridley 25; NASA: 7; Peter Newark's Pictures: 14; PhotoDisc: Scenics of America 4; Jeremy Woodhouse 13b; Popperfoto: Reuters/Mike Segar 27b; U.S. Army Corps of Engineers: Peter Shugert 16; Westchester County Office of Tourism, White Plains, New York: 24

Printed in the United States of America

1 2 3 4 5 6 7 8 9 07 06 05 04 03

# Table of Contents

# Gateway to the Northeast

*The Hudson River is the largest and most important river in the state of New York. Along with a system of canals, the river joins New York City to the Great Lakes and the Midwest.*

From its origin as a tiny, lake-fed stream in the Adirondack Mountains, the Hudson River flows in a southward direction. It then heads between the Catskill Mountains and the Taconic Mountains, widening and deepening into a tidal estuary (river mouth) 150 miles (241 kilometers) long. Finally, it enters New York Harbor and flows through the Verrazano Narrows into the Atlantic Ocean.

### River Traffic

Along with its main tributary, the Mohawk River, the Hudson has always been an important inland waterway. Native Americans who lived along its banks for thousands of years before the arrival of Europeans traveled the river in canoes. The Europeans first arrived on the river early in the seventeenth century. Merchant ships sailed up the Hudson as far north as what is

now the city of Albany to load valuable cargoes of furs that were then taken back to Europe.

In the nineteenth century, canals were built to link the Hudson with the Great Lakes so that barges could travel between the Midwest and New York City. The barges brought supplies, such as metal tools, to the people of the Midwest. The barges then carried the products of midwestern farms and factories back through the Hudson Valley to New York City and other ports along the river.

## Quieter Times

Today, the canals are used mainly by pleasure boats instead of barges, but oceangoing ships from all over the world still sail up the Hudson

**Left:** *Near the mouth of the Hudson River, the Statue of Liberty stands overlooking New York Harbor and the New York City skyline.*

**Right:** *The mansion of Frederick Vanderbilt is one of several grand houses built by wealthy American families beside the Hudson River.*

to the New York cities of Newburgh, Poughkeepsie, Kingston, and Albany. New York City, once a small Dutch fort on the southern tip of the island of Manhattan, has grown into one of the largest and most prosperous cities in the world.

The Hudson Valley is an important industrial and farming region. In the past, pollution from factories and farms damaged the river. The pollution harmed the fish that lived in the river and the birds and other animals that fed on the fish.

By the 1960s, the Hudson had become one of the most polluted rivers in the United States. The amount of pollution has now been reduced, however, and the river is getting cleaner. Today, tourists from all over the United States, Canada, and other countries come to the Hudson to enjoy its spectacular scenery and visit its historic sites.

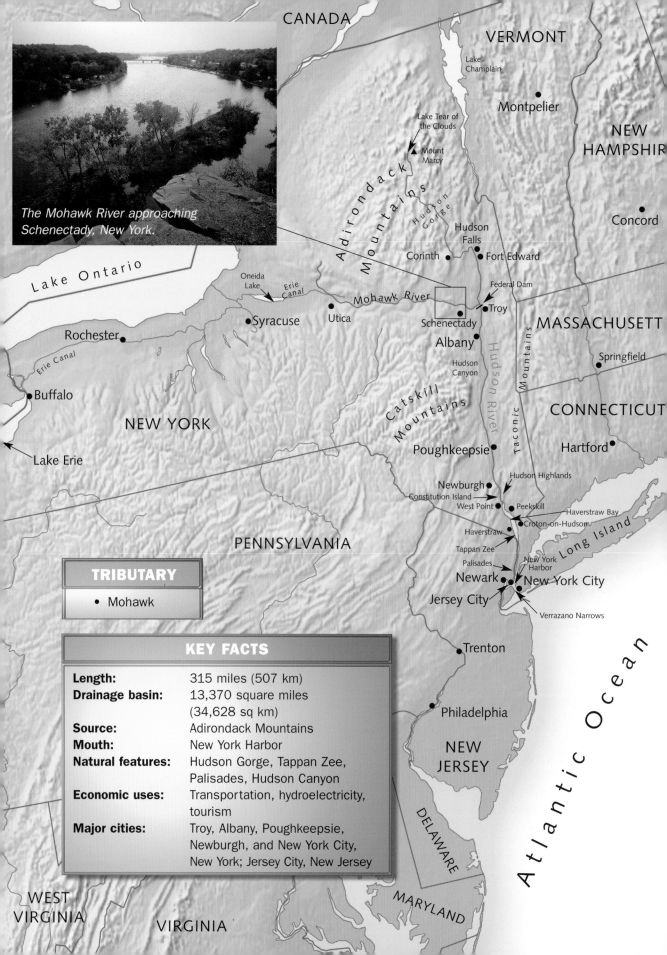

CANADA

VERMONT

Lake Champlain

*The Mohawk River approaching Schenectady, New York.*

Montpelier

NEW HAMPSHIR

Lake Tear of the Clouds

▲ Mount Marcy

Concord

Adirondack Mountains

Hudson Gorge

Hudson Falls

Corinth

Fort Edward

Lake Ontario

Oneida Lake

Erie Canal

Federal Dam

Mohawk River

Troy

MASSACHUSETT

Syracuse

Utica

Schenectady

Albany

Rochester

Erie Canal

Hudson Canyon

Taconic Mountains

Springfield

CONNECTICUT

Buffalo

NEW YORK

Catskill Mountains

Hudson River

Hartford

Lake Erie

Poughkeepsie

Hudson Highlands

Newburgh

Constitution Island →

West Point

Peekskill

Haverstraw Bay

Croton-on-Hudson

PENNSYLVANIA

Haverstraw

Tappan Zee

Long Island

Palisades →

New York Harbor

Newark

New York City

Jersey City

Verrazano Narrows

Trenton

Philadelphia

NEW JERSEY

Atlantic Ocean

DELAWARE

WEST VIRGINIA

VIRGINIA

MARYLAND

## TRIBUTARY

- Mohawk

## KEY FACTS

| | |
|---|---|
| **Length:** | 315 miles (507 km) |
| **Drainage basin:** | 13,370 square miles (34,628 sq km) |
| **Source:** | Adirondack Mountains |
| **Mouth:** | New York Harbor |
| **Natural features:** | Hudson Gorge, Tappan Zee, Palisades, Hudson Canyon |
| **Economic uses:** | Transportation, hydroelectricity, tourism |
| **Major cities:** | Troy, Albany, Poughkeepsie, Newburgh, and New York City, New York; Jersey City, New Jersey |

# From Source to Mouth

*From its headwaters in a small lake, the Hudson swings through mountain ranges and plunges through rapids and gorges before reaching the ocean through a broad, forest-fringed valley.*

From its source high in the Adirondack Mountains, the Hudson River travels 315 miles (507 km) south through New York state to its mouth in New York Harbor. It drains 13,370 square miles (34,628 sq km) of land, which is about the size of the neighboring states of Massachusetts and Connecticut combined.

## Cloudy Course

The source of the Hudson is Lake Tear of the Clouds, a little teardrop-shaped pond about the size of a football field. It lies on the southwest slope of Mount Marcy, the highest mountain in New

**Above:** *A picture of the mouth of the Hudson River taken from a satellite. Millions of people live in New York City and other towns in this area.*

### PARKS AND FORESTS

- Adirondack Park
- Bear Mountain State Park
- Catskill Park
- Harriman State Park
- Hudson Highlands State Park
- Liberty State Park
- Saratoga National Historical Park

York State. From there, the Hudson winds through mountains and thick forests to the town of Hudson Falls.

During its journey through the Adirondacks, the Hudson is a fast-flowing stream. Fed by creeks and lakes, it plunges over rapids and waterfalls and through gorges. The most spectacular is the 13-mile (21-km) Hudson Gorge, which is a favorite spot for rafters.

The Hudson widens as it flows southeast past Corinth, then heads northeast to Hudson Falls. At Hudson Falls, the river turns south and leaves the Adirondacks at Fort Edward. Between Fort Edward and Troy, the number of towns on the Hudson's banks increases. Just north of the town of Troy, the Hudson is joined by its only major tributary, the Mohawk River, which flows in from the west.

### Tidal Valley

Below Federal Dam at Troy, the Hudson River flows through a beautiful, steep-sided valley for 150 miles (241 km) to New York Harbor and the Atlantic Ocean. The valley was carved through the surrounding mountains by a glacier. This happened during the last Ice Age, which ended about twelve thousand years ago. When the ice melted, the ocean flooded into the valley. Today, the valley continues along the seafloor for about 200 miles (322 km) to New York Harbor. This undersea section is called the Hudson Canyon.

Downstream from Troy, the Hudson River is tidal—its level rises and falls twice a day as the ocean tides wash in and out of the river's mouth. The freshwater flowing down the Hudson meets and mixes with the saltwater coming in from the Atlantic. This makes the Hudson's water salty 60 miles (97 km) upstream from the ocean.

### Narrows and Lakes

From Troy, the Hudson flows south past Albany, which is a major river port and the state capital of New York. The river flows past

**Below:** *A view across the Hudson River from Bear Mountain State Park at the southern end of the Hudson Highlands*

Poughkeepsie to Newburgh between the Catskill Mountains on its west and the Taconics on its east.

South of Newburgh, the river enters the Hudson Highlands, where thickly forested hills line both banks for 15 miles (24 km). Along this stretch, the Hudson is narrow, fast-flowing, and deep. The deepest point on the whole river—216 feet (66 meters)—is here between Constitution Island and West Point.

The Hudson River leaves the highlands at Peekskill. It narrows again, then broadens into Haverstraw Bay. This bay is about 6 miles (10 km) long, and here the Hudson looks more like a lake than a river. From Croton-on-Hudson across to Haverstraw, the river is 3 miles (5 km) wide—the broadest point on the river.

## Heading for the City

At Croton Point, the Hudson passes from Haverstraw Bay into another wide stretch named Tappan Zee. This 9-mile (14-km) section is 2 miles (3 km) wide. The river narrows again as it leaves Tappan Zee and flows toward New York Harbor and the ocean.

From this point, the river forms part of the boundary between New York and New Jersey. On the New Jersey side, sheer sandstone cliffs called the Palisades rise to a height of more than 500 feet (152 m) as the river approaches New York City.

New York Harbor marks the end of the Hudson's journey. At the southern end of the harbor, the river passes through the Verrazano Narrows and flows into the Atlantic Ocean.

# 2 The Life of the River

*The thick forests and clear waters of the Hudson River Valley support a large amount of wildlife. The area's natural beauty attracts many people, but in the past, pollution damaged the environment.*

The Hudson River receives its water from plentiful supplies of rain and winter snows. In the mountains, the winters are often severe, while areas farther south enjoy milder weather. Plants grow easily in the region's good soil, and much of the land is covered by thick forests.

The river's forests are home to many small animals, such as skunks, chipmunks, and raccoon, as well as a few larger predators, including coyotes and black bears. Cottontail rabbits thrive on the region's farmlands. Muskrat, river otters, mink, and beavers live on the banks of the many small creeks that flow into the Hudson. Along the banks and in the riverside marshes, plants such as reeds and cattails shelter insects, fish, and water birds.

## Problem Plant

Some plants on the Hudson River are less useful to the river's wildlife. Water chestnuts grow in thick masses in many parts of

**Above:** *This blue crab is one of the many sea creatures that live in the Hudson's estuary, where the river water and seawater mix together.*

the Hudson and the Mohawk Valleys, choking many of the other water plants in the river. People brought this fast-growing plant to the United States from Asia in the nineteenth century. They used it to decorate ponds and lakes. In the 1860s, however, some of it escaped from a lake in New York state and got into the Mohawk River. It then steadily spread along the Mohawk and into the Hudson. Another foreign plant, named the floating heart, is spreading in the waters upstream of Troy. Environmental workers are attempting to wipe out these invading plant pests.

## Amphibians and Reptiles

Many amphibians live along the river's banks and in its marshes. Amphibians are animals that live both on land and in the water. The Hudson River's amphibians include several types of frogs, such as the green frog and the spring peeper, and the rare mudpuppy salamander.

River reptiles include garter snakes, which often feed in the marshes but usually prefer to stay on dry land. The northern water snake, however, does swim in the river itself. Diamondback terrapins are another common reptile, and snapping turtles feed

**Below:** *A diamondback terrapin withdraws its head into its shell. This species is the only type of American turtle that survives in tidal rivers like the Hudson.*

on plants growing in the river mud, sometimes gulping down small fish and straggling ducklings.

## Fish and Birds

More than two hundred types of fish have been found in the Hudson River. In the freshwater part of the river above Newburgh, the fish include largemouth and smallmouth bass, catfish, trout, pike, bullheads, perch, crappies, and carp. Farther downstream, where the water is salty, there are shad, herring, striped bass, bluefish, flatfish, yellow eels, seahorses, and even a few sturgeons.

Other creatures in the Hudson's long stretch of salty water include jellyfish, blue crabs, lobsters, and mollusks, such as clams and mussels. The zebra mussel spread from the Great Lakes to the Hudson River in 1991. Carried on the bottom of cargo ships, this shellfish is now taking over large areas of the riverbed. The mussels have become pests, because they take living space from the local types of mollusks.

### ATLANTIC STURGEON

The largest fish in the Hudson River is the Atlantic sturgeon (below). This fish can grow to 14 feet (4.3 m) long and weigh up to 800 pounds (363 kilograms), but the sturgeons in the Hudson are usually less than half that size. The Atlantic sturgeon spends most of its time at sea but enters large rivers such as the Hudson to breed. Sturgeons are caught for their eggs, known as caviar, and dense meat, which was once called Albany beef, but overfishing (too much fishing) has greatly reduced their number.

## POISON IN THE RIVER

The Hudson River has been badly polluted in the past because of the many factories, farms, and cities along its banks. Today, people are more careful about what they put in the river, and this is making the water much cleaner, but some pollutants are difficult to remove. The most harmful of these are chemicals called PCBs (polychlorinated biphenyls). These were once used in electric appliances and in paints and plastics. In 1977, it was discovered that PCBs were poisonous, and laws were passed to prevent people from making them. By that time, however, huge amounts of PCBs had already collected in the Hudson's mud. Health officials still advise people not to eat fish caught in the Hudson River until the PCBs can be completely eliminated from it.

**Right:** Fishers in an unpolluted creek in the Taconic Mountains. Fish in the Hudson itself are not fit to eat.

Like other rivers, the Hudson is home to many ducks, geese, and gulls. Kingfishers, sandpipers, herons, egrets, and yellowlegs, plus ospreys, bald eagles and other birds of prey also live there. Small perching birds, such as marsh wrens and yellow warblers, live in the river's marshes near the mouth. Grouse, woodcocks, and quail are plentiful on the land near northern parts of the river.

Many of the birds seen along the Hudson are just temporary visitors. This is because the Hudson is an important flyway—a route taken by migrating birds. Geese and ducks follow the river when flying south in winter and north in summer, when they head to their breeding grounds in Canada.

**Left:** An osprey returns to its perch with a fresh catch. Ospreys live along the entire length of the Hudson Valley.

# River of Many Nations

*The fertile Hudson Valley has been home to many people over the years. Several Native American groups in the area gave way to the wave of European settlements in North America.*

The first people to live on the lands along the Hudson were Native Americans. They arrived to the area thousands of years ago and lived by hunting, fishing, and gathering fruits, nuts, and roots. Later on, they added to their food supply by growing crops, such as sunflowers, corn, squashes, pumpkins, and beans. They typically lived in large, rectangular-shaped, wooden buildings called longhouses.

## The Great River

When the first European settlers arrived in the seventeenth century, the people living along the Hudson were mostly Mohicans, Wappingers, Delawares, and Mohawks. The Mohicans had forty villages between the Catskill Mountains and the southern end of Lake Champlain. The Mohicans called themselves the *Muhhekunneuw*, meaning "people of the great river." The "great river" was the Hudson. Their largest village was near what is now the city of Albany, the capital of New York State.

The Wappingers lived in about thirty villages on the east side of the Hudson.

**Below:** *A painting of a Mohawk chief from the early eighteenth century.*

Their territory extended south from the Taconic Mountains to the Atlantic coast.

The Delawares, also known as the Lenapes, controlled land from present-day Delaware to Long Island.

The Mohawks lived in just three villages near what is now Schenectady, New York, on the Mohawk River, which was named for them. The Mohawks called themselves the *Kahniankehaka*, which means "people of the flint," but other tribes called them the Mohowaanuck, which means "man eaters." The Europeans shortened *Mohowaanuck* to Mohawk.

## Arrival of the Dutch

The first European to visit the Hudson River was Italian explorer Giovanni de Verrazano. He sailed his ship into the mouth of the river in 1524, but he did not travel far upstream. For the rest of the sixteenth century, the only European visitors to the region were pirates and slavers, who would often raid Native villages around the river mouth to steal valuables and to capture slaves.

The first European to explore the Hudson River itself was English explorer Henry Hudson. In 1609, he sailed up the river that now bears his name and made contact with the Wappingers and Mohicans. Hudson was working for the Dutch, who began settling along the Hudson in the 1620s. In 1624, they built Fort Orange, the first permanent European settlement in New York, which is now the city of Albany. They also began settling on the southern tip of Manhattan Island, where they built a fort that soon became surrounded by the village of New Amsterdam.

In 1626, the governor of

### HENRY HUDSON

The Hudson is named for English explorer Henry Hudson, the first European to sail up the river. In 1609, Dutch merchants asked Hudson to find a water route from Europe to China. He sailed along the Atlantic coast of North America looking for a channel through to the Pacific Ocean. The channel he chose to follow turned out to be just a river, not a passage to the Pacific.

**Above:** *Henry Hudson, with his ship in the background, is greeted by Native people beside the Hudson River.*

New Amsterdam bought Manhattan from the local Native people. This small group of Natives was called the *Manhattans* or "people of the island." Their payment for the island was metal tools, jewels, and weapons. It is likely the Manhattans did not understand that this sale would include their being forced to leave their land.

By 1629, Dutch settlers began building towns along the Hudson Valley. Many places in the region, such as the Bronx, Rensselaer, and Cohoes, still have their original Dutch names, as do the Catskill Mountains.

At first, the Dutch got along well enough with the Native residents, and they traded with them for furs and other products. Soon, however, there were arguments about who owned the land along the sides of the river. Many Native people also suffered badly from diseases brought from Europe, such as influenza, smallpox, and typhus, to which they had no immunities.

**Below:** *A view of the U.S. Military Academy beside the Hudson at West Point. Army officers have been trained at this facility for more than two centuries.*

## ARRIVING IN THE UNITED STATES

Ellis Island is located in New York Harbor very near the Statue of Liberty and a few miles upstream from the mouth of the Hudson River. In 1892, the island became a reception center for the thousands of immigrants who arrived in New York City every year. For more than sixty years, Ellis Island was the first piece of U.S. soil on which twelve million new arrivals set foot. Immigrants were examined by doctors and questioned by officials on the island to decide who would be allowed onto the mainland. The center closed in 1954, and today it is a museum.

**Below:** *New arrivals outside the main reception building on Ellis Island in 1907.*

## Military Maneuvers

In the 1660s, the British began taking control of the Hudson Valley away from the Dutch. In 1664, the New Amsterdam governor, Peter Stuyvesant, surrendered his town to a British fleet without a fight. The British changed the name of New Amsterdam to New York, and what had been Fort Orange became Albany.

British control of the region did little to help Native people. The Native groups frequently found themselves involved in wars between European powers, often fighting on both sides. These wars included the conflict between Britain and France for

**Above:** *A 1909 photograph shows the warehouses and piers along Manhattan's West Street with the Hudson beyond. Both river barges and oceangoing ships arrived here to load and unload cargoes.*

control of North America in the 1750s, and later the American Revolution.

The Hudson Valley played a vital role in the American Revolution (1775–1783), when Americans broke free from British rule. It was the scene of important battles at Saratoga Springs (1777) and Tappan Zee (1781). George Washington, commander of the American forces and later the first president of the United States, set up his headquarters at Newburgh

in 1782. West Point, which is on the banks of the river, was a key American fort during the Revolution. Now, the fort is home to the U.S. Military Academy.

## Trade Boom

Throughout the nineteenth century, the Hudson and Mohawk Rivers were connected to a network of canals. This network linked the Great Lakes and the Midwest with ports on the Hudson. Coal, grain, and timber from the Midwest were carried in barges to the ocean for loading onto ships in New York Harbor.

The canals boosted the economy of the region, and millions of people came to the area to work. Immigrants mainly came from Europe, especially Ireland, Poland, and Italy, arriving in New York City. Some of the new arrivals moved north to work on farms and in new factories beside the Hudson. Many stayed in New York City, which has been the largest city in the United States since 1790.

New York City originally covered only the island of Manhattan. But in 1898, it grew to include the boroughs of Brooklyn, the Bronx, Queens, and Staten Island. Today, eight million people live in the city itself, and a further thirteen million live in the huge sprawl of suburbs that surrounds the city and the lower section of the Hudson River, spreading into New Jersey and Connecticut.

## THE WORLD'S FIRST STEAMBOAT

The world's first successful steamboat—the *Clermont* (below)—was designed by U.S. engineer Robert Fulton. It was built in New York City and launched on the Hudson River in 1807. The vessel had two side paddle wheels powered by a steam engine. On its first voyage, the *Clermont* traveled from New York City to Albany. The 151-mile (243-km) journey took just thirty-two hours. The sailing ships used on the river at that time, called sloops, needed four days to make the same journey.

# 4 From Freight to Fun

*The Hudson and its canals once formed the most important cargo network in the United States. Today, the waterways are much quieter but are quite popular with tourists.*

Furs were a big attraction for the first European settlers of the Hudson Valley. In the early seventeenth century, Dutch ships sailed from the Hudson to the Netherlands laden with beaver, otter, mink, and wildcat skins. This valuable trade brought many new settlers to the valley. The settlers cleared the trees from large areas of land in order to build houses and create fields for growing crops and grazing cattle.

## Early Industry
The river was the main highway for the Europeans settling the region. The Europeans' boats carried

**Above:** *A harbor filled with yachts on the New Jersey side of the Hudson River across from midtown Manhattan. The Hudson is the chief waterway in the New York City area.*

products from towns along the Hudson Valley to the port of New York City. From there, ships carried these products all over the world.

The Hudson was also a source of power. Paddle wheels, turned by the flowing river, drove mills that cut timber, made paper, and ground wheat into flour. By the early nineteenth century, waterwheels were also powering ironworks and other factories. These made the Hudson Valley an important manufacturing center. Many of these older industries are now gone from the area. High-tech companies manufacturing computers, electronic equipment, and medical products have taken their place, but logging and papermaking are still major industries along the upper stretches of the Hudson.

The river also powers generators that produce electricity. Today, much of the Hudson Valley's electricity comes from hydroelectric plants at dams on the river. These dams—the largest being Federal Dam near Troy—help stop the river from flooding.

## Cargo Traffic

The Hudson's importance as a trade route increased rapidly in the nineteenth century when a canal was built to link it to the Great Lakes. The population of this territory was growing fast at the time because it contained timber, valuable minerals, and large areas of fertile farmland.

In 1816, DeWitt Clinton, the governor of New York, suggested digging a canal to link Lake Erie to the Hudson River. It would run from Buffalo, New York, which is on Lake Erie, along the Mohawk Valley to the Hudson just north of Troy.

**Above:** *A cargo boat on the Erie Canal passes grain-filled silos at Buffalo, New York, in 1926.*

**Below:** *A containership heads out to sea, passing under the Verrazano Narrows Bridge across the mouth of the Hudson*

Instead of traveling for weeks overland, people and freight would be able to sail quickly and easily between New York City and the Midwest. The Erie Canal opened in 1825. Shipping freight from the Midwest to New York City took just nine days, and the canal became a success. Within fifteen years, New York City had risen from being the fifth-largest port in the United States to the largest.

### Barge Canal

Throughout the nineteenth century, a great deal of time and money was spent building, maintaining, and adding to the canals. The Erie and other canals were constructed to run around obstacles in the rivers, such as rapids. The Hudson's canal system had to be enlarged twice so that it could accomodate larger and larger barges.

Then, at the beginning of the twentieth century, engineers decided to stop digging so many artificial channels. Instead, they tamed the Hudson and Mohawk Rivers so that barges could use them safely. Stretches of the rivers were deepened, and dams and locks were built to control the levels of water. The whole system was finished in 1918 and renamed the New York State Barge Canal.

The Barge Canal was a major transportation network for most of the twentieth century, but it slowly lost business as

companies began to send freight by road or rail. The opening of the St. Lawrence Seaway in 1959 spelled the end of the Hudson's canals. The St. Lawrence Seaway allowed oceangoing ships to travel between the Atlantic Ocean and the Great Lakes. There was no longer any need for cargo to travel by barge along the Erie Canal to Albany or New York City for loading onto ships.

## Modern Routes

Freight is now carried in trucks along highways, such as the New York State Thruway, which run parallel to the old barge route. From New York City, this freeway heads north, up the Hudson Valley to Albany, then west along the Mohawk Valley to Buffalo. Most passenger traffic along the Hudson Valley also travels on highways and railroads.

The Hudson River is crossed by several bridges. These include the George Washington Bridge, which joins Upper Manhattan to Fort Lee, New Jersey; the Tappan Zee Bridge, near Tarrytown, New York; and the Newburgh-Beacon Bridge further north. Road and rail tunnels under the river link New York City to cities in New Jersey.

Many freight barges have

### WINE MAKING IN THE HUDSON VALLEY

The Hudson Valley contains some of the oldest vineyards in the United States. A vineyard is a place that grows grapes for making wine. French immigrants planted the first Hudson vineyards in 1677 in what is now Ulster County near the Catskills. Most of the wine they made was for their own use rather than for sale. These vineyards appeared one hundred years before the first ones were planted in California. The first commercial winery in the Hudson Valley opened in 1837 at Washingtonville. Still in use, it is the nation's longest-working winery. Today, there are more than twenty wineries in the Hudson Valley.

**Above:** *A vintner (wine maker) picks grapes from a vine growing beside the Hudson River.*

disappeared from the canal system, but some ships and barges still travel on the river. These shipping vessels carry a wide range of cargo, including sand, stone, fuel, timber, steel, and grain. Oceangoing ships can travel upstream as far as Albany. The port at Albany can handle vessels up to 750 feet (229 m) long.

## New Industries

Almost all the traffic on the canal system now consists of pleasure boats. Pleasure boating and other tourist activities are major industries in the Hudson Valley and the Adirondack Mountains. Millions of tourists visit the region every year to spend time boating, fishing, and hiking. They also visit the many museums, parks, historic houses, and other sites such as West Point military academy and the world-famous Statue of Liberty.

Much of the scenic beauty of the Hudson River comes from its mountains and forests, and more than half of the land in the Hudson River Basin is forested. About a quarter of the river basin is used for farming, and less than a tenth is covered by towns and cities. The region's farms produce fruit such as apples and grapes, meat and dairy products, eggs and poultry, and wheat, sweet corn, flowers, and onions.

## A Major Population Center

The major cities along the Hudson River and its canals include the New York cities of Troy, Schenectady, Albany, Poughkeepsie, and Newburgh. Many of these places, especially Albany, have busy river ports. One

**Above:** *A leisure boat takes tourists on a cruise along a stretch of the Hudson River north of New York City.*

of the biggest population centers anywhere in the world, however, is at the river's mouth. About 21 million people live in the greater New York City area, which includes Jersey City and Newark, New Jersey, and many other towns that spread across much of New Jersey, Connecticut, and Long Island. Flowing down the western side of New York City, the Hudson River is a major landmark for New Yorkers and visitors alike.

## ALBANY

The city of Albany (below), on the Hudson River 143 miles (230 km) north of New York City, is the capital of New York State. It began as Fort Orange, a base for Dutch fur traders in 1624, but it soon became an important transportation center. In the late eighteenth century, it was a popular staging post for the pioneer wagon trains taking settlers to the Midwest.

The city became even more prosperous when the Erie Canal opened in 1825 and when the first railroad in the state—from Albany to Schenectady—opened in 1831. In 1919, Albany built one of the first commercial airports in the United States, and in 1932, it opened docks that were large enough to handle oceangoing ships. Today, the city's population is about 96,000. It has a busy port, and its industries include engineering and papermaking.

**Below:** *Empire State Plaza in the center of Albany with the New York State Capitol in the distance. The rounded building on the right, nicknamed the "Egg," is an arts center and auditorium.*

**Above:** *Traffic whizzes through the Lincoln Tunnel, which travels under the Hudson River to join Manhattan to Union City, New Jersey.*

The natural harbor at the river's mouth made the city the center of trade, industry, and tourism it is today.

Most of the trade and transportation facilities at the lower end of the Hudson are run by the Port Authority of New York and New Jersey. The Port Authority operates the docks, which handle about 130 million tons (118 million tonnes) of cargo per year. Every year, about 3 million tons (2.7 million tonnes) of cargo and 90 million passengers pass through the authority's airports—Newark and Teterboro in New Jersey and La Guardia and Kennedy airports in New York City. The authority also operates the Lincoln and Holland Tunnels under the river, three bridges, bus and rail lines, and truck terminals.

As in the Hudson Valley and the Adirondack Mountains to the north, tourism is a large industry in the New York-New Jersey region, which attracts about 35 million visitors a year from other parts of the United States and the world.

## HUDSON FERRIES TO THE RESCUE

Following the attacks on the World Trade Center in lower Manhattan on September 11, 2001, hundreds of thousands of people who worked in the towers or lived in the surrounding districts needed to get away from the area. All were frightened and many were injured. With subway trains suspended and many roads blocked, the ferry boats that crisscross the nearby Hudson River came to their rescue. Throughout that terrible day, at least 200,000 people were taken to safety across the river to ferry terminals in Hobokon and Jersey City, New Jersey.

Many of the ferry terminals in the district were damaged when the towers collapsed, and the ferry crews had to load passengers wherever they could tie up. Some of the ferries were used as water ambulances, taking two thousand injured firefighters to hospitals across the river.

**Below:** *A Hudson River ferry passes behind the ruin of the World Trade Center. On the day of the attack, ferries took thousands of survivors to safety.*

# 5 Places to Visit

*The Hudson River flows through a variety of beautiful landscapes and passes many important historic sites.*

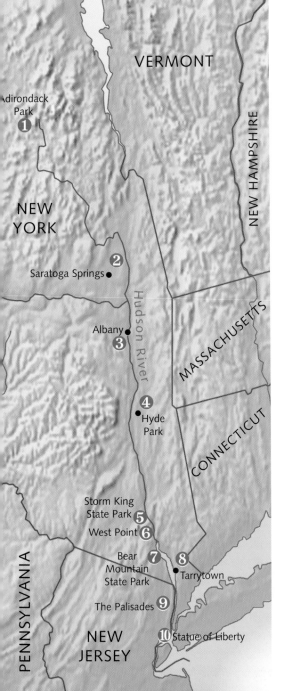

**① Adirondack Park, New York**
Adirondack Park is a wilderness area of mountains, forests, rivers, and lakes. Visitors come in summer to hike, camp, fish, ride horses, bike, canoe, and whitewater raft. Winter sports enthusiasts can ski, skate, dog sled, and snowmobile.

**② Saratoga Springs, New York**
Situated in the foothills of the Adirondacks, Saratoga Springs is a good place for outdoor activities such as hiking, fishing, and boating. Its other attractions include its famous racecourse, a historical museum, and the Saratoga Battlefield from the American Revolution.

**③** *West Point, From Pillipstown by William James Bennett*

**③ Albany Institute of History and Art, Albany, New York**
The Hudson River School of painters was the first group of American landscape painters. The artists painted mainly in and around the Hudson River Valley, such as at West Point (above), during the middle of the nineteenth century. The Albany Institute of History and Art has one of the world's finest collections of the group's paintings.

### ❹ Hyde Park, New York

At Hyde Park, 20 miles (32 km) south of Kingston, a clifftop path overlooks the river that leads past the historic houses of financier Ogden Mills, President Franklin D. Roosevelt, and industrialist Frederick Vanderbilt. Nearby is the former home of President Roosevelt's wife, Eleanor. These houses and their gardens are open to the public.

### ❺ Storm King State Park, New York

This state park is the northern gateway to the steep Hudson Highlands south of Newburgh. The mountain itself is 1,355 feet (413 m) high, and its walking trails give spectacular views of the river.

### ❻ West Point, New York

Home of the U.S. Military Academy, West Point features a free museum, restored fortifications, and other historic sites. West Point stands on a high bluff, providing great views of the Hudson Valley.

### ❼ Bear Mountain State Park, New York

Situated just 50 miles (80 km) north of New York City, opposite Peekskill, this mountain earned its name because it resembles a bear lying down.

### ❽ Tarrytown, New York

The leafy, historic village of Tarrytown has many historic buildings and churches, and its museum illustrates the history of the Hudson Valley. The nearby village of Sleepy Hollow was made famous by Washington Irving's novel *The Legend of Sleepy Hollow*, a frightening tale about a headless horsemen (right).

### ❾ The Palisades, New Jersey

These cliffs along the west bank of the Hudson River in New Jersey and New York soar to a height of more than 500 feet (152 m). Visitors can see the cliffs from the New York City side of the river.

### ❿ The Statue of Liberty, Liberty Island

Ferries from the southern tip of Manhattan carry people to the Statue of Liberty in New York Harbor. The statue is one of the best-known symbols of the United States.

**Above:** *Tourists arrive on the Liberty Island ferry to take a closer look at the 302-foot-high (92-m) statue and enjoy views of New York Harbor.*

# How Rivers Form

*Rivers have many features that are constantly changing in shape. The illustration below shows how these features are created.*

Rivers flow from mountains to oceans, receiving water from rain, melting snow, and underground springs. Rivers collect their water from an area called the river basin. High mountain ridges form the divides between river basins.

Tributaries join the main river at places called confluences. Rivers flow down steep mountain slopes quickly but slow as they near the ocean and gather more water. Slow rivers have many meanders (wide turns) and often change course.

Near the mouth, levees (piles of mud) build up on the banks. The levees stop water from draining into the river, creating areas of swamp.

① **Glacier:** An ice mass that melts into river water.

② **Lake:** The source of many rivers; may be fed by springs or precipitation.

③ **Rapids:** Shallow water that flows quickly.

④ **Waterfall:** Formed when a river wears away softer rock, making a step in the riverbed.

⑤ **Canyon:** Formed when a river cuts a channel through rock.

⑥ **Floodplain:** A place where rivers often flood flat areas, depositing mud.

⑦ **Oxbow lake:** River bend cut off when a river changes course, leaving water behind.

⑧ **Estuary:** River mouth where river and ocean water mix together.

⑨ **Delta:** Triangular river mouth created when mud islands form, splitting the flow into several channels called distributaries.

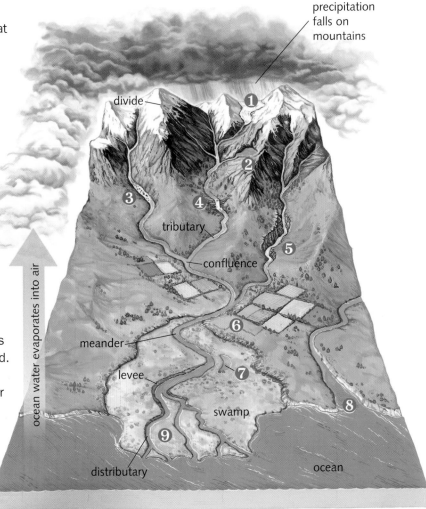

# Glossary

**barge** A flat-bottomed boat used to transport goods and usually pulled or pushed by a tug.

**basin** The area drained by a river and its tributaries.

**borough** A section of a city or town that may have its own government, such as the Bronx in New York City.

**canal** A manmade waterway used for navigation or irrigation.

**dock** A place where ships load and unload.

**freshwater** Inland water that is not salty.

**generator** A machine that turns mechanical energy into electricity.

**gorge** A narrow, steep-sided valley or canyon.

**harbor** A sheltered area of water deep enough for ships to anchor.

**hydroelectricity** Electricity made by generators driven by flowing water.

**immigrant** A person who moves to another country from his or her native land.

**ironworks** A place where iron is made from iron ore or where iron objects are made.

**mollusks** A type of shellfish that includes mussels and clams.

**rapids** Shallow parts of a river where the water runs very fast.

**saltwater** Seawater or other bodies of water that are salty.

**tidal** Rising and falling water levels that occur because of tides.

**tributary** A river that flows into a larger river at a confluence.

**waterway** A river or canal that boats can travel on.

**whitewater** The fast-flowing, frothy water of rapids and waterfalls.

# For Further Information

## Books

Dwyer, Michael Middleton. *Great Houses of the Hudson River*. Bulfinch Press, 2001.

Lourie, Peter. *The Hudson River: An Adventure from the Mountains to the Sea*. Boyds Mills Press, 1998.

Parker, Steve. *Eyewitness: Pond and River*. DK Publishing, 2000.

Whitcraft, Melissa. *The Hudson River*. Franklin Watts, 1999.

## Web Sites

*Historic Hudson River*
www.hhr.highlands.com

*Hudson River: An American Treasure*
www.marist.edu/summerscholars/99

*Hudson River Foundation*
www.hudsonriver.org

*New York Hudson's Valley's Information Resource*
www.hudsonriver.com

# Index